COUGARS

Sandie Lee Books

Cougars

Cougars are large wild cats that are also known as pumas, mountain lions and panthers. The cougar is the fourth largest wild cat. It is the second biggest in the Americas. There are 5 different species of the cougar found today. The cougar is closely related to the cheetah. Many cultures have used the cougar to represent power. In this article we are going to explore the many cool facts about cougars. So let's get started.

Where in the World?

Did you know cougars have the widest range of all the big cats? Cougars are highly adaptable; however, they do prefer to stay hidden. For this reason they will roam the mountains and dark forests. They can be found from the Yukon in Canada, to the Andes in South America.

The Body of a Cougar

Did you know a male cougar can grow to be around 220 pounds? A cougar can range in color from dark brown to tawny red. It has white markings on its throat, chest, chin and whiskers. The body of a cougar is very muscular and powerful and it has a very long tail.

The Cougar's Eyes

Did you know the cougar's eyes can be amber or green in color? The cougar uses its powerful eyesight to hunt for prey at dusk and at night. The eyes of a cougar are set close together, this allows it to have better vision. The eyeball itself is also bigger than most carnivores.

The Cougar's Paws

Did you the paw print a cougar makes is called a "pug mark"? The paw of the cougar is adapted to not only climbing but for running. The long sharp claws of the cougar are retractable. This means it can pull its claws back into its paw. It uses its sharp claws to take down prey.

What a Cougar Eats

Did you know cougars only eat meat? Cougars are purely carnivores. The cougar hunts deer, coyotes, raccoons and other mammals big and small. If a cougar takes down a large animal, it will feast on it for several days. It is very protective of its kill and will guard and even hide its prey from other animals.

The Cougar's Special Ability

Did you know the cougar is a great jumper? The cougar has very powerful back legs. It can jump 18 feet straight up in the air. The cougar can leap forward at 29 feet and also run very fast. This animal has reached speeds up to 34 miles-per-hour for short distances.

The Cougar as a Predator

Did you know the cougar hunts alone? The cougar hunts with stealth. It will stalk its prey until the perfect time arrives. The cougar then rushes at its prey and pounces on its back. From here it will bite down around its neck, dragging it to the ground, then carry it off.

The Cougar as Prey

Did you know that cougars have no natural enemies except for man? The cougar has been hunted for trophies by man for many years. In some regions, the cougar was hunted until there was not any left. Farmers have also killed cougars because they are a threat to their livestock.

Cougar Talk

Did you know cougars use several different sounds to communicate? Unlike a pet cat, cougars do not meow, but they do make various sounds. Cougars can growl, hiss, scream, yowl and even purr. Baby cougars tend to make soft chirping sound with their mother. Cougars will also scent mark their territories.

The Cougar Mom

Did you know the mother cougar can have anywhere from 1 to 6 cubs? To find a mate, the female cougar will rub her scent on trees. This attracts a male cougar. The mother cougar is pregnant for 84 to 106 days. During this time, she will look for a safe and sheltered place to have her cubs.

Baby Cougars

Did you know baby cougars are born with spots? These spots help keep the cubs camouflaged and safe from predators. The cubs are born helpless and will feed milk from their mother until they are about 6 weeks old. After this the mother will bring her cubs meat from a kill.

Cougars at Rest

Did you know cougars make what are called, daybeds? A cougar will make a bed for itself to rest and to keep warm and dry. These beds can be in a cave, a shallow nook or even a rocky outcrop. Some cougars will also sleep in forested areas or under fallen trees and thickets.

Cougars at Play

Did you know cougar cubs play to learn to hunt? Adult cougars live a solitary life, but the cubs do play. After the cubs are walking, they begin to play with each other. They will practice stalking, pouncing and leaping with their littermates. Cubs will also play with their mother's tail. This helps them develop good hunting skills.

Life of a Cougar

Did you know female cougars live longer than male cougars? Male cougars can live up to 12 years-old in the wild. The male cougar is also constantly travelling. His territory range can be anywhere from 50 to 150 miles. He will defend his territory by fighting off other male cougars.

Quiz

Question 1: What other names are the cougar known by?

Answer 1: Mountain lion, puma and panther

Question 2: What color is the cougar?

Answer 2: It can be tawny to dark brown. It has white markings on its face, throat and chest.

Question 3: What is the footprint of a cougar called?

Answer 3: a "pug" mark

Question 4: A cougar can run 34-miles-per-hour. What other strong ability does it have?

Answer 4: A cougar can leap forward up to 29 feet in a single bound.

Question 5: How does a female cougar attract a mate?

Answer 5: She rubs her scent on trees

Thank you for checking out another addition from Sandie Lee Books! Make sure to check out Amazon.com for many other great titles.